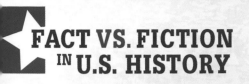

FACT VS. FICTION IN U.S. HISTORY

THE LEWIS AND CLARK

EXPEDITION:
SEPARATING FACT FROM FICTION

by Matt Chandler

CAPSTONE PRESS
a capstone imprint

Introduction

William Clark could not believe his eyes. He and his men had been traveling for a year and a half in search of the Pacific Ocean. They traveled thousands of miles. They were hungry, tired, and homesick. Finally, on November 7, 1805, they saw the wide ocean in the far distance. Clark wrote in his journal, "Great joy in camp we are in view of the ocean, this great Pacific Ocean which we been so long anxious to see."

Fact!

Lewis brought his dog, Seaman, on the expedition. Seaman was the only animal to make the entire journey and return home.

Lewis and Clark sailed down the Missouri River during the first part of their journey.

But Clark and the explorers were not looking at the ocean. What they saw was the mouth of the Columbia River. It is one of many **myths** told about this historic trip to explore the western **frontier**. More than 200 years after the Lewis and Clark expedition, many myths remain about this epic journey. Let's separate fact from fiction.

Chapter One

The Louisiana Purchase

In 1803, President Thomas Jefferson purchased more than 800,000 square miles (2,071,990 square kilometers) of land from France. This deal is known as the Louisiana Purchase. Today, this land covers part or all of 15 U.S. states from Louisiana to the Pacific Coast. President Jefferson wanted to find a water route to the West. Transporting supplies by water meant the western land could more easily be developed.

The president called upon his friend and former secretary, Meriwether Lewis, to lead an expedition he called the Corps of Discovery. Lewis had served in the military with a man named William Clark. He chose Clark to help him lead the expedition.

Meriwether Lewis

William Clark

Thomas Jefferson

The expedition began on May 14, 1804, in St. Louis, Missouri. The Corps of Discovery had about 45 members. Clark had brought along a Black man he enslaved named York. The other members were white. It has long been said that they were the first white men to explore the new land. But that is a myth. Animal trappers and traders had explored the western frontier before the expedition members.

The expedition was also promoted as a scientific mission. The group did identify 178 different plants. But its main purpose wasn't science. The Corps of Discovery was a military mission to find a waterway to make moving west easier. That is why President Jefferson chose military men to lead the group.

A page of Clark's diary from the expedition shows a sketch of an evergreen shrub leaf.

Chapter Two

The Indigenous People

The historical accounts of the expedition often focused on Lewis and Clark as the men who made the trip possible. They were the leaders and **navigators**. The story was told that they were mapping and traveling **uninhabited** land. That was a myth. Indigenous tribes had lived on the land for many years. They had traveled back and forth across the same routes Lewis and Clark "discovered."

Many experts believe the trip would have never been possible without the help of the Indigenous people. Lewis and Clark met as many as 50 different Indigenous **tribes** on their journey. The Indigenous people helped the explorers hunt. They fed the explorers during the winters when food was limited. The Indigenous people shared their knowledge of the land. Lewis and Clark were great explorers. But they owe much to the Indigenous tribes.

FOREVER CHANGED

Without the Indigenous people, the expedition likely would have failed. Yet in the years after they returned, the American government did a lot to hurt the Indigenous tribes.

Using the maps Lewis and Clark created, there were many expeditions west. Soon, traders were occupying the new territory. The government passed many laws hurting Indigenous people. One was passed in 1830 called the Indian Removal Act. It forced Indigenous people from their land to give it to the settlers.

Lewis and Clark greet Indigenous people on their journey.

How Dangerous Was the Trip?

Exploring the new territory was dangerous. The explorers faced bad weather. They encountered snakes, bears, and other wild animals. Even though the danger of the trip was real, there were plenty of myths. The group brought more than 200 pounds (91 kilograms) of gunpowder. They carried weapons that included an air rifle. Jefferson believed the expedition members might have to fight off woolly mammoths and giant sloths. The reality of the danger was quite different than the fears before they left. There were no woolly mammoths or giant sloths.

Woolly mammoths were a type of elephant. Scientists think they died out in North America between 10,500 and 7,600 years ago.

Expedition members did use their weapons against members of the Blackfeet Nation. At least one member of the Blackfeet Nation was killed.

Expedition members carried several rifles and other weapons to use for defense and to hunt for food.

Chapter Three

The Expedition Journals

Much of what is known about the expedition comes from the journals kept by Lewis, Clark, and other expedition members. They wrote about 1 million words during the trip. The plan was for Lewis to write a book detailing the journey once the group returned. Like many parts of the expedition, not everything was as it seemed.

Some researchers have said parts of the journals were **plagiarized**. They were taken from the works of other writers and explorers of the time. Also, Lewis never wrote his planned book. He claimed to suffer from writer's block. He died in 1809, just three years after the expedition returned, and never completed the project. It wasn't until 100 years later, in 1905, that the complete journals were published.

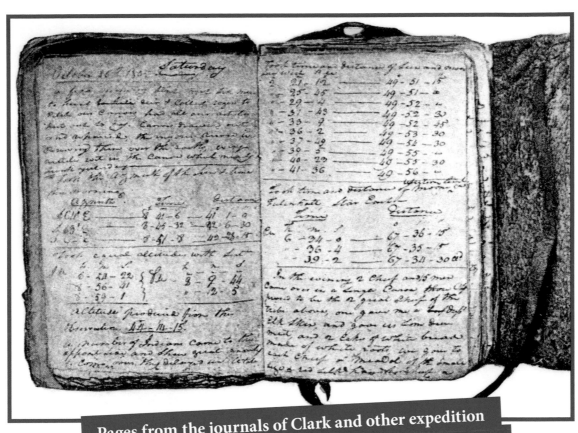

Pages from the journals of Clark and other expedition members help people remember their journey today.

Chapter Four

Sacagawea, York, and a Vote

For more than 100 years, there was a myth that Sacagawea, a member of the Shoshone, played an important role in the expedition as the guide. Her role was reported as being critical to the success of the trip.

The interpretations of Sacagawea (standing in right boat with her arms extended) helped the members of the expedition and Indigenous people communicate.

Sacagawea was the wife of Toussaint Charbonneau, a French-Canadian fur trader. He had lived among Indigenous people for a long time. He knew a lot about their traditions and language.

Both Charbonneau and Sacagawea were **bilingual**. They served as **interpreters** between Lewis and Clark and Indigenous people. In the journals of Lewis and Clark, it was written that Sacagawea was good at gathering food. She also helped ease the tension between the Indigenous people and the expedition members. Still, she was not critical to the group's success the way that history remembered her.

A VALUABLE MYTH?

It may have been a myth that Sacagawea played a major role in the expedition. But that myth inspired millions of women. The myth led to advances in women's rights. For example, she has been honored for advancing women's right to vote. In 2000, the U.S. government issued a gold $1 coin with Sacagawea and her baby on the front.

The Voting Myth

One of the most famous myths is about a vote the members took in November 1805. The expedition needed to build a camp for the winter. They were near the Columbia River in Washington State. The group had different options. They could cross the river and set up camp on the other side. Or they could travel the river in both directions looking for the best place to build their camp. If they made the wrong decision, they could starve or freeze during the long winter.

Sacagawea was pregnant when she joined the expedition. She gave birth during the trip.

On November 24, 1805, Lewis and Clark gathered the members to cast a vote on where to build the camp. As the story was told, Sacagawea and York were allowed to vote. In the years since then, this vote has been called the first time a woman and a Black person were allowed to vote in the United States.

The vote resulted in the group staying at Fort Clatsop near the mouth of the Columbia River during the winter of 1805.

In the early 1900s, women fought for the right to vote in the United States. They used the tale of Sacagawea voting to inspire the fight. But many historians argue it wasn't a formal vote. Some sources question whether Sacagawea and York's votes were even recorded. Even if they were, it wasn't a historical vote. Some women and Black people were allowed to vote in the state of New Jersey as early as 1776.

Sacagawea and York were important members of the expedition. But they did not make history on that November day in 1805.

Fact!

According to the journals of Lewis and Clark, York went on a buffalo hunt with other members of the expedition in December 1804. He and some of the other men returned with frostbite.

Women and others stand in line to vote in New Jersey after the state's constitution allowed them to vote in 1776.

Chapter Five

Returning Home

The expedition returned home to St. Louis on September 23, 1806. Today, Lewis and Clark are seen as American heroes. Yet the men failed in their primary mission—to find a waterway connecting the Missouri River to the Pacific Ocean. No such waterway existed. For the next 150 years, their story was mostly forgotten.

Lewis, Clark, and the other expedition members make their way down the Missouri River.

John Charles Frémont

Lewis and Clark were forgotten partly because they didn't immediately publish the book detailing their trip. Eventually, other explorers mapped the West, including John Charles Frémont. The more Frémont and others were talked about, the more Lewis and Clark's trip was forgotten.

It wasn't until the 1960s when interest in the expedition was renewed. Modern historians learned about the expedition. People then wrote about Lewis and Clark as heroic explorers.

Fact!

Large chunks of the journey are not recorded. The journals were either lost or the men did not write during these times.

Freedom for York?

In the time of Lewis and Clark, it was common for white men to enslave Black people. The enslaved people were often kidnapped. They were beaten, threatened with death, and forced to work.

York worked alongside the members. In their journals, Lewis and Clark wrote that York played an important role. He hunted for food. He scouted the best routes to travel. He **bartered** with the Indigenous people.

A myth told for many years said that once they returned home, Clark granted York his freedom. Years later, when some of Clark's family papers were discovered, it was revealed that he kept York as an enslaved man for at least another 10 years.

★ Fact!

In 2001, President Bill Clinton recognized York's role in history by **posthumously** naming him an honorary sergeant in the U.S. Army.

Today, a statue honoring York
stands in Louisville, Kentucky.

Chapter Six

Life After the Expedition

President Jefferson knew the expedition wasn't a huge success. But he pretended it was, creating another myth. He even rewarded Lewis and Clark by giving them each 1,600 acres (647 hectares) of land and double pay for their work. Others in the expedition received double pay and land too. As an enslaved person, York got nothing for his work.

Lewis was named governor of Upper Louisiana Territory. But instead of building on his success, Lewis fell deep in debt. He suffered from depression, and he died when he was just 35 years old. Jefferson named Clark a brigadier general and Indian agent of the Louisiana Territory. Clark eventually published a partial account of the expedition in 1814. After Lewis and Clark returned, many explorers, trappers, and traders followed their path west to explore the new land.

By following Lewis and Clark's routes, trappers and traders had a better chance of survival in the American West.

The retelling of the expedition has led to many myths. But that doesn't mean Lewis and Clark weren't brave. Every member of the expedition showed great courage to explore the new land. They may not have succeeded in mapping a water route to the West, but they did complete the journey. Many historians still see the expedition as an important event in America during the 1800s.

In 1954, a U.S. postage stamp came out to remember the 150th anniversary of the expedition's departure.

Timeline

1803	President Thomas Jefferson asks Congress for $2,500 to fund an expedition of the West with hopes of mapping a waterway to the West. The mission would be led by Lewis and Clark.
December 20, 1803	The Louisiana Purchase is completed.
May 14, 1804	The expedition begins in St. Louis, Missouri.
August, 20, 1804	Sgt. Charles Floyd dies. He is the only expedition member to die during the trip.
November 11, 1804	Sacagawea joins the expedition at its camp in North Dakota.
November 15, 1805	The expedition reaches the mouth of the Columbia River at the Pacific Ocean.
September 23, 1806	The expedition ends in St. Louis.

Glossary

barter (BAHR-tuhr)—to trade food or goods and services instead of using money

bilingual (bye-LING-wuhl)—the ability to speak two languages with equal or near equal ability

frontier (fruhn-TIHR)—the far edge of a settled area, where few people live

interpreter (in-TUHR-pruh-tuhr)—a person who hears one language and translates its meaning to another

myth (MITH)—a false idea that many people believe

navigator (NAH-vuh-gay-tuhr)—a person who uses instruments and charts to find their way

plagiarize (PLAY-juh-rize)—to steal and pass off the ideas or words of another as one's own

posthumous (PAHS-chuh-muhss)—happening after death

tribe (TRYB)—a group of people who share the same language and way of life

uninhabited (uhn-in-HAH-buh-tuhd)—not lived in

Read More

Buckley, James, Jr. *Sacagawea: Courageous Trailblazer!* San Diego, CA: Portable Press, 2021.

Davis, Hasan. *The Journey of York: The Unsung Hero of the Lewis and Clark Expedition*. North Mankato, MN: Capstone, 2019.

Micklos, John, Jr. *Lewis and Clark's Compass: What an Artifact Can Tell Us about the Historic Expedition*. North Mankato, MN: Capstone, 2021.

Internet Sites

History.com: Lewis and Clark Expedition
history.com/topics/westward-expansion/lewis-and-clark

National Archives: Lewis & Clark Expedition
archives.gov/education/lessons/lewis-clark

National Geographic Kids: America Heads West
kids.nationalgeographic.com/history/article/lewis-and-clark

Index

About the Author

Matt Chandler is the author of more than 80 books for children and thousands of articles published in newspapers and magazines. He writes mostly nonfiction books with a focus on sports, ghosts and haunted places, and graphic novels. Matt lives in New York.